First Facts®

You Can Write

# You Can Write an Amazing Journal

by Jennifer Fandel

**Consultant:**
Terry Flaherty, PhD
Professor of English
Minnesota State University, Mankato

CAPSTONE PRESS
a capstone imprint

First Facts is published by Capstone Press,
1710 Roe Crest Drive, North Mankato, Minnesota 56003.
www.capstonepub.com

*Library of Congress Cataloging-in-Publication Data*
Fandel, Jennifer.
  You can write an amazing journal / by Jennifer Fandel.
      p. cm. — (First facts. You can write)
  Summary: "Introduces readers to the how-tos of keeping a journal through
the use of examples and exercises"—Provided by publisher.
  Includes bibliographical references and index.
  ISBN 978-1-4296-8408-8 (library binding)
  ISBN 978-1-4296-9318-9 (paperback)
  ISBN 978-1-6206-5260-2 (ebook PDF)
  1. Diaries—Authorship—Juvenile literature.  I. Title.

PN4390.F36 2013
808.06'692—dc23                                         2012003762

**Editorial Credits**
Jill Kalz, editor; Sarah Bennett, designer; Kathy McColley, production specialist

**Photo Credits**
Dreamstime: Corachaos, 12; Shutterstock: Artush, 8, bendao, 9 (timer), Blaj Gabriel, 11 (girl),
Boobl, 7 (book), 10 (book), 14 (book), 16 (book), Chas, cover (pen), Danny E Hooks, 16 (ticket),
dedMazay, 18 (bear), JGade, 19 (frog), Johan W. Elzenga, 15, Jonathan G, 16 (sky), jumpingsack,
cover, (zombie) 10, (zombie), karakotsya, 7 (doodle) Keith Publicover, 17, luckypic, 6, Luis
Santos, 3, mashe, 11 (orange), Matthew Benoit, 14 (bug on leaf), Mike Flippo, 13, Nazzu, 14
(trees), oksana2010, 22, Orla, 16 (feet), Otna Ydur, 5, Photo Grafix/Black Rhino Illustration, 18
(cookie), rSnapshotPhotos, 20, Sergej Khakimullin, 9 (pencil), Thomas M Perkins, 21, Zinaida,
19 (sky)

**Artistic Effects**
Shutterstock: Albert Campbell, oldm, Marilyn Volan

Printed in China.
032012      006677RRDF12

# TABLE of CONTENTS

My Journal

# A Place of Your Own

Imagine your own private place. A place where you can do anything you want. You can yell. You can sing. You can work out problems or daydream about the future.

A journal is such a place. And you can carry it with you wherever you go. It's all yours. You are free to write whatever you wish. Your journal is a **collection** of your everyday thoughts.

**collection**—a group of things gathered together

5

Journals take many forms. You might use a notebook and a pencil. Or a blank hardcover book and a pen. Or a computer. Pick a journal that makes you feel like writing.

Be sure to add the date before writing each day. Dates will help you keep track of what you wrote and when.

For one day, carry your journal everywhere. Anytime you have a thought, write it down. At the end of the day, look at what you wrote. Do you see any patterns? What kinds of things did you write about most?

November 22

Supposed to snow today. Hope so! Wearing my lucky mittens to school.

Surprise quiz in math.

I think I want to be a chef when I grow up. I love food!

Why won't it snow?! We better get some before Thanksgiving.

**FAST FACT**

The word "journal" comes from the French word for day. A journal is for all types of daily writing. A diary is different. It's usually for private thoughts and secrets only.

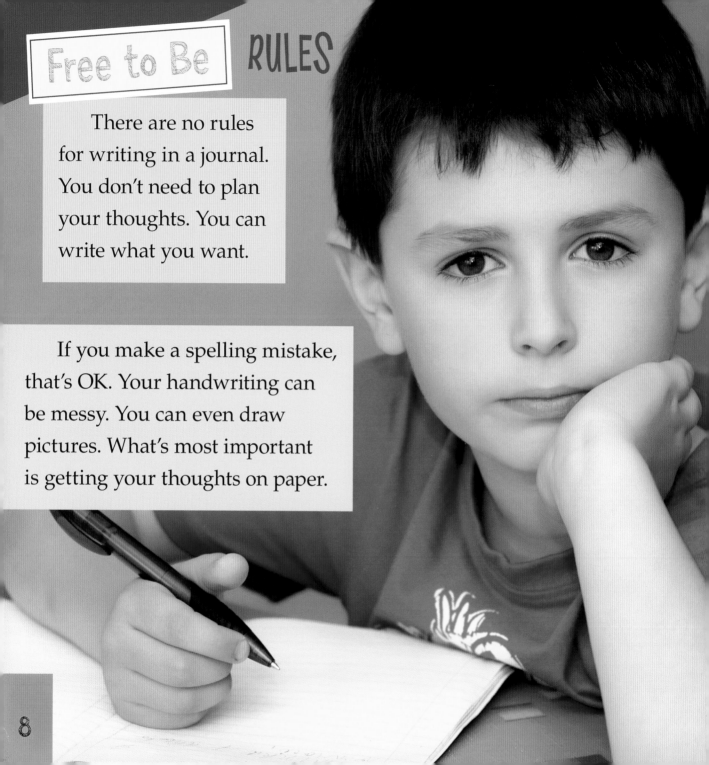

# Free to Be RULES

There are no rules for writing in a journal. You don't need to plan your thoughts. You can write what you want.

If you make a spelling mistake, that's OK. Your handwriting can be messy. You can even draw pictures. What's most important is getting your thoughts on paper.

Free writing is a great way to get ideas on paper. Set a timer for 10 minutes and go! Write everything that pops into your head. Don't think. Don't worry about rules. If you get stuck, try this: Write a sentence like "My pencil is magic!" over and over until a new thought comes to you.

*My pencil is magic!*

*My pencil is magic!*

*...nagic!*

# MAKING TIME

Make writing in your journal a **habit**, like brushing your teeth. Try writing at the same time every day. It'll help you remember to write.

Every day has something interesting or surprising in it. What did you like about the day? What did you dislike? How did people or events make you feel?

April 16

Last night I dreamed a zombie ate my homework! I was the last person picked for kickball today too. That never happens. Made me feel sad. Dad made pancakes tonight. Looked funny, but tasted great!

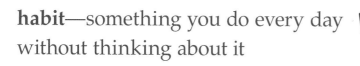

**habit**—something you do every day without thinking about it

Pick one moment that sticks out in your day, and write about it. Maybe someone shared her orange with you at lunch. How did that make you feel? How did it taste? What happened afterward? If she hadn't shared, how would your day have been different?

# TAKING NOTES

A journal is a good place for **observations**. Think of yourself as a reporter. Watch activities in a backyard or park. Watch people at school or the mall. Use your five senses to record the world around you.

**What do you see?**

**Hear?**  **Taste?**

**Smell?**  **Touch?**

I saw a boy with purple hair.
I heard a bird say twiddle-dee-doo.
I smelled someone grilling burgers.
The park bench I sat on was hard.

**observation**—something you see or take in with your other senses

# Exercise

Create a journal about one subject, such as dreams or sports. For a dream journal, write down everything you can remember about your dreams. Be sure to include colors, smells, names, or sounds. For a sports journal, write about sports you play or watch.

**FAST FACT**

Some people keep nature journals. They write about plants and animals they see. They may even make drawings to help them remember what they saw.

Facts swirl around you every day. You read books. You learn new things at school. Your parents tell you something you didn't know. What do you do with all of this knowledge? Write it down!

There's a buzzing sound in the trees. Mr. Lind told me it's a bug. A cicada. I found a dead one, and it looked spooky.

In your journal you can ask questions and then do **research**.

Today Mom said that the Inuit have 100 words for snow. Really? What are those words? I need to look them up.

**research**—to study and learn about a subject

Make a "wondering" list. Write down five things you want to know more about. The moon? Elephants? Airplanes? Pick your favorite idea and research it at the library or on the Internet. Ask a teacher or librarian for help.

# SAVING THINGS

**Images** and objects that fill you with strong feelings can also go inside your journal. Photos, maps, and ticket stubs are a few examples. They can help you remember special moments.

I feel best when the setting sun is **bright pink** ... when I hear the **thunk-thunk** of a basketball ... when I smell pizza ... when I feel sand on my bare feet.

**image**—a picture

16

Paste a picture you like in your journal. Maybe it's a photo you took of your cousin. Or a magazine ad. Or a cartoon your sister drew. Write about it. What do you see? Why is it so special? How does it make you feel?

## Be Creative STORYTELLING

Use your journal to jot down ideas for stories, plays, or poems. Note things you see. Write down words you hear. A journal is a good place to work on your storytelling skills. It's a safe place to play with words, sounds, and thoughts.

### POEM

The round bear
broke the cookie jar.

The round bear cried boo-hoo.

His round mom said
no more dessert,

no more for you-know-who.

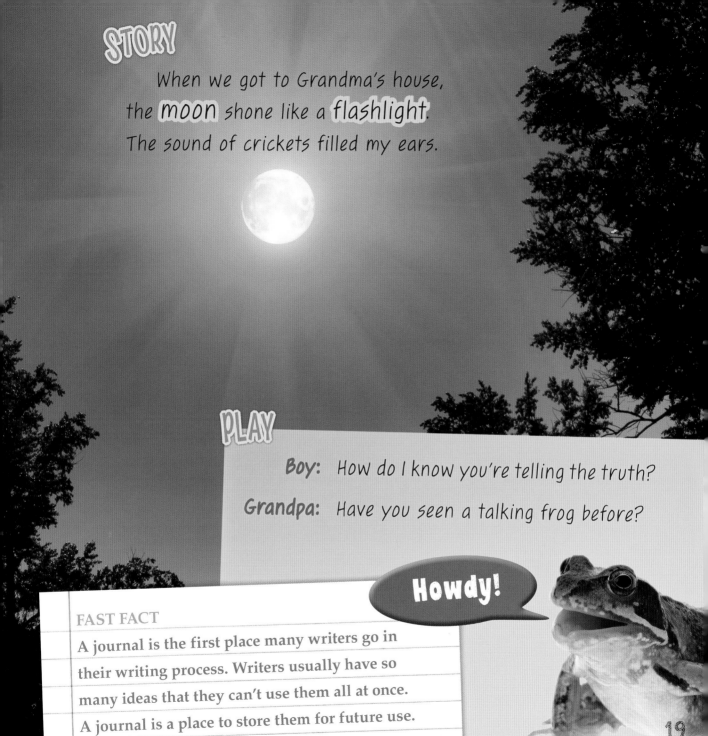

## STORY

When we got to Grandma's house,
the **moon** shone like a **flashlight**.
The sound of crickets filled my ears.

## PLAY

**Boy:** How do I know you're telling the truth?

**Grandpa:** Have you seen a talking frog before?

Howdy!

**FAST FACT**

A journal is the first place many writers go in their writing process. Writers usually have so many ideas that they can't use them all at once. A journal is a place to store them for future use.

19

# SAFEKEEPING

Your journal is always ready to be written in, day or night. And it gives back to you every time you read it. You can find ideas you forgot you had. You can see problems you worked out.

You can discover how much you've learned.

## A journal is a journey.

Your thoughts go
somewhere every day.
So write them down!
Where will yours
take you?

# GLOSSARY

**collection** (kuh-LEK-shuhn)—a group of things or objects that are gathered over a long period of time

**habit** (HAB-it)—something you do every day without thinking about it

**image** (IM-ij)—a picture

**observation** (ob-zur-VAY-shuhn)—something that you have noticed by watching carefully

**research** (REE-surch)—to study and learn about a subject

# READ MORE

**Loewen, Nancy.** *It's All about You: Writing Your Own Journal.* Writer's Toolbox. Minneapolis: Picture Window Books, 2009.

**Mack, Jim.** *Journals and Blogging.* Culture in Action. Chicago: Raintree, 2009.

**Minden, Cecilia, and Kate Roth.** *How to Write a Journal.* Language Arts Explorer Junior. Ann Arbor, Mich.: Cherry Lake Pub., 2011.

# INTERNET SITES

FactHound offers a safe, fun way to find Internet sites related to this book. All of the sites on FactHound have been researched by our staff.

Here's all you do:

Visit *www.facthound.com*

Type in this code: 9781429684088

Super-cool stuff!

Check out projects, games and lots more at
**www.capstonekids.com**

# Index